LOVE GOD AND LOVE YOUR NEIGHBOR, THAT WILL FIX EVERYTHING

James D Bethel

ISBN-13: 9798418464576
ISBN-10: 8418464577

Cover design by: Art Painter
Library of Congress Control Number: 2018675309
Printed in the United States of America

I would like to thank my loving wife Jean for allowing me the time that it took to put together this essay. I would also like to thank my wonderful daughter Katelyn for helping edit my work. And mostly, I would like to thank God for the inspiration and clarity to put it into writing.

INTRODUCTION

After writing two fiction action novels, God seemed to be pushing me in a new direction. I'm not sure if he was telling me to expand my repertoire, or if he just wanted me to use some of my college education. Regardless, I am taking a shot at writing a non-fiction essay. I graduated from The Ohio State University in 1991 with a Bachelor of Science in Education. At least that's what the diploma hanging in my office says on it. My goal was to teach social studies in junior or senior high school. I had taken countless hours of history classes in college and was ready to "mold young minds", or at least that was my plan. I got married two weeks after graduation and expected someone to hand me a teaching job. I was surprised to find out that securing a job teaching social studies was not an easy chore. "I worked hard to earn my degree, so they owed me a job, right!"

I became frustrated and began looking elsewhere to start a career. I'm a married man after all, and that was what I was supposed to do. After a year of odd jobs, my father-in-law told me that the U.S. Postal Service was hiring mail carriers. My wife's family had worked for the Postal Service for several generations and were doing alright for themselves, so I applied. Within a few weeks I had gone through my training and was out on the street, delivering mail. Life quickly took off from there for us; we had a new house built and started a family. I realized that a career of teaching history was well in my rear-view window.

I continued to use my teaching skills as a Sunday school

teacher at the Salvation Army. Moving forward to today, I have taught teenagers for thirty some years now. I hope I have changed or improved some lives along the way. There have been times when I was provided a curriculum to teach from, and others when I did it all on my own (well with God's help, obviously). I always thought it was important to relate to the students at their level and understand where they were in their lives. Along the way, my wife and I raised two incredible children of our own.

Through my many years of teaching generations of teens, I have learned to try and simplify the Bible into terms the kids could relate. I am realistic enough to know that in today's fast paced environment, few teens are going to spend hours studying their Bible. I have learned to break the complexity of the Bible down to something easier to swallow and understand. I tell the students that the entire Bible can be summed up by my favorite verses. Mark 12:30-31 reads, "Love the Lord your God with all your heart and with all your soul and with all your mind and with all your strength. The second is this: Love your neighbor as yourself. There is no commandment greater than these."

I had years of studying history in college, and many more witnessing it in my daily life. I have also spent plenty of time studying my Bible and teaching Sunday school. For me, these verses have never seemed more valuable than they do today. If we are going to move forward in a better direction as humans, we need to put these verses into action.

CHAPTER 1

LOVE THE LORD

In the Gospel of Mark, Jesus was tested by one of the "teachers of the law". He asked Jesus what he thought the most important commandment was. Jesus knew the man was trying to test him and responded in Mark 12:30-31: "Love the Lord your God with all your heart and with all your soul and with all your mind and with all your strength. The second is this: Love your neighbor as yourself. There is no commandment greater than these."

However far Jesus was pushed, he was always willing to go a step further. The teacher asked him for the greatest commandment, so he gave him two. I think Jesus was trying to emphasize what God had been saying for thousands of years in the Bible. Jesus was using the kiss method (keep it simple stupid). He was telling everyone that God had been saying this all along, but we have made it overly complicated. God told us in the original ten commandments to "love God and love your neighbors". If we follow those simple directions, everything else will work out.

I tried to simplify the Old Testament when I taught my students in Sunday school. When you study the Old Testament, the same pattern was repeated. God's people would turn away from him and seek their own way and bad things always happened. They would lose wars, get enslaved, or face natural disasters. They would eventually be led to turn back to God and seek forgiveness. He would restore them and sooner or later, the cycle would be repeated. Fortunately for them, God's grace is not like ours. We would probably have given up on them and counted them as lost. Not only did God not give up on His people, but he also ended up sacrificing his only Son for them. It seems like a good time to remind everyone of John 3:16, "For God so loved the world that he gave his one and only Son, that whoever believes in him shall not perish but have eternal life." That would be the perfect definition of true love.

In the beginning of times, God gave the people the ten commandments through Moses. If you study Exodus 20 closely enough, you will see that this was one of the first times we were taught to love God first and then love our neighbor. The first four commandments tell us to love God: "1 You shall have no other gods before me, 2 You shall not make idols, 3 You shall not take the name of the Lord your God in vain, 4 Remember the sabbath day and keep it holy." These commandments focused us on loving, honoring, and respecting God first.

The final six commandments took us in a different direction. They dealt mainly with our relationships with our fellow humans. "5 Honor your father and mother, 6 You shall not murder, 7 You shall not commit adultery, 8 You shall not steal, 9 You shall not give false testimony against your neighbor, and 10 You shall not covet your neighbors (possessions)". In Exodus 20:12-17, God was detailing, through Moses, the idea of loving your neighbor. He started specifically with loving our father and mother, meaning your own household. He then, turned his focus outside of our front door. Referring to our neighbors, He said, don't kill them, lust after them, steal from them, lie about them, or want their stuff. God tried to make it simple enough, so the people would not look for loopholes. He gave us a detailed list on how to love God and love your neighbors.

Moses died before the Israelites made it into the "promised land". They were led into their future homelands by Joshua. Before he allowed the tribes to disperse into their separate regions, he felt he needed to remind them: "But be very careful to keep the commandment and the law that Moses, the servant of the Lord gave you: to love the Lord your God, to walk in all his ways, to obey his commands, to hold fast to him and to serve him with all your heart and all your soul." (Joshua 22:5) The Israelites had been through many trials and battles since Moses had brought them the ten commandments. Joshua wanted to impress on them one final time to love God first. A few chapters later in the book of Joshua, he leaves them with his own personal testimony. It is one of my favorite verses, as he gives them a choice. "But if serving the Lord seems undesirable to you, then choose for yourselves this day whom you will serve, whether the gods your forefathers served beyond the river, or the gods of the Amorites, in whose land you are living. But as for me and my household, we will serve the Lord." (Joshua 24:15) He is once again reminding them that God is not forcing them to love him. He led them to the "promised land" that he had guaranteed to their ancestors, but he gave them free will to make the choice on their own. We are also free to make the same choice of loving God and putting him first in our lives.

Loving the Lord with all your heart might seem impossible. God knows that it is a difficult task for us. He understands that we have many flaws, and he is willing to see past them. He just asks that we give him our whole heart as best as we can and love him. King David was a great example of a flawed human who was still loved by God. The prophet Samuel pointed out that David was "a man after His (God's) own heart." (1st Samuel 13:14) This would make us think that David must have been as close to perfect as anyone could be. Anyone who followed David's life history knows better.

After David became king, he lusted after a married woman named Bathsheba. He slept with her, and she became pregnant. Once David found out, he began to put together a scheme to cover up his sin. He first tried to get her husband to immediately sleep with her, so he would think he was the cause of her pregnancy. When Uriah would not do it, he moved on to "Plan B". He had Uriah placed at the most dangerous part of the ongoing war. It did not take long for Uriah to be killed in battle.

Let that sink in. This incredible leader, "a man after God's own heart", had a man killed to cover up his own sin. I would have to imagine that very few of us have committed such a grievous sin, but this was not the end of King David. After Nathan pointed out David's sin to him, he admitted "I have sinned against the Lord". (2nd Samuel 12:13-14) Nathan promised David that "the Lord has taken away your sin".

That is how much the Lord loves us! He simply wants us to show the same love to him. Throughout the Book of the Psalms, David confesses his love for God. Psalm 18 is a great example of it: "I love you, O Lord, my strength. The Lord is my rock, my fortress and my deliverer." David writes and sings throughout the Book of the Psalms about his love for the Lord. The same God who had enough grace and love for him to see past his sins.

We often find ourselves blaming God for our problems. We wonder where he was, when we were in a valley of despair or at the end of our rope. I've been there. I might not have been in a valley as deep as you feel like you are in, but I have had my days too. God might seem so very far away from you, even now. I promise you that he did not move away from you. We are the ones who do the moving away. Just like the Israelites did throughout the Old Testament. God is within an arm's length, ready to embrace you back from your sin and disobedience. He has not left you or forsaken you. He has been with you throughout your despair. He is just waiting patiently for you to call upon him for help.

CHAPTER 2

ALL YOUR HEART

The easiest way to love God with all our heart is to follow the scriptures. In Mark 12:30-31, Jesus reminded us to begin by giving God our whole heart. If you think back to your childhood, you can easily remember how important your heart was. We were taught that it was the most important organ in the human body. If it stopped working, so did we. Even as young children, we knew we had to protect our hearts. Jesus explained to his disciples in Matthew 18:3, "I tell you the truth, unless you change and become like little children, you will never enter the kingdom of heaven." God is telling us to have faith like children and give your heart back to the one who created it.

As teenagers, we were willing to give our heart to our current crush and get it broken again and again. Luckily for us, God made our hearts strong enough to handle that kind of abuse. If you are patient enough, and follow God's leading, you might find someone who will value your heart and help you protect it. God wants us to give him our whole heart. He wants us to trust him to return just the right amount of our heart to share with the world.

When thinking about the heart, I think back to the countless time someone lost a game or didn't finish a project. I can hear it in my head, "He just didn't have his heart in it." We use it as an excuse to fail. Life is not nearly that simple. In this example we are normally saying that someone failed because they were not dedicated or committed to a mission. God wants us to give our heart to him and not use it as an excuse to fail. If you know me well enough, you expect a "Rocky" reference here. I won't let you down. During the movie "Rocky III", while he is training to fight Mr. T, Rocky appears distracted and shows a lack of interest. Apollo Creed is frustrated by his inadequate effort, so Adrian confronts Rocky. He admits to her that he is afraid that he is going to screw up and lose everything they have. She tells him that she is willing to walk away from everything they have gained to keep him. The material possessions are meaningless. He needs to believe in himself and put his heart into his training, because she believes in him. And of course, as in every "Rocky" movie, everything changes immediately. He becomes focused and (spoiler alert) he wins.

God's telling us the same thing. He believes in us! We need to give him our whole heart and he'll help us work everything else out. So how do we give God our whole heart? It's not like the game of Operation. We can't just pluck it out with those little tweezers. In Psalm 51:2, David asks God to "wash away all my iniquity and cleanse me from my sin." We first need to ask God for forgiveness. Believe it or not, that is the easy part. The hard part for most of us is, believing that he has forgiven us for our sins. We find it impossible to believe that God really forgave us. We keep reminding ourselves of our past failures and sins. We are not willing to move clear of our own past. We need to trust God and move on. If King David, with his checkered past, was willing to believe that he was forgiven, then we should too. Later in the Book of the Psalms 51:10, David asks God again to, "create in me a pure heart, O God. And renew a steadfast spirit within me."

A steadfast spirit like Rocky was what he meant. He needed to believe again. Believe that God has moved on and forgiven him. That's what we need to do too. Trust God's forgiveness and believe that things, and life, can change for us. We also need to ask the Holy Spirit to search our hearts and burn up any sin within it. Then, we will be able to offer God our whole heart. And when you feel inadequate and have fallen short, and its going to happen, go back to step one and ask God for forgiveness.

So, do you have to go to church to find this level of forgiveness? No, not necessarily, but it does help being around people who are on the same journey. I've heard many people tell me that they can't go to church until they have cleaned up their life. They fear that the people in the church will judge them for their past. I fear that that is a problem that churches have created for themselves, with too many judgmental members. As a church member, I need to make sure that everyone feels God's love flowing from me, not judgement. God doesn't stand at the church door only allowing perfect people inside. He asks us to come as we are and allow him to perfect us. One of the best scripture prayers you can say to help with this is Psalm 139:23-24. "Search me, O God, and know my heart; test me and know my anxious thoughts. See if there is any offensive way in me and lead me in the way everlasting."

One of my favorite examples of a person with a "good heart" is Buck O'Neil. Buck was easily one of the most genuine kindhearted men to walk the earth. He was a first baseman and manager in the Negro American League. He spent most of his playing career with the legendary Kansas City Monarchs. His life is detailed in a wonderful book by Joe Posnanski called "The Soul of Baseball". After his Negro League time, Buck became a scout for the Chicago Cubs in 1955. He was later named the first black coach in the Major Leagues with the Cubs.

He was instrumental in the founding of the Negro League Baseball Museum in Kansas City. If you are interested in hearing about baseball from a man who has seen it firsthand, find one of his interviews on YouTube. I can remember sitting in my car outside of a store, unable to turn the radio off, because he was telling the broadcaster some of his stories. He faced incredible obstacles and never had the opportunity to play in the Major Leagues. He did not let it get him down but expressed thanks for his time in baseball. He was a man who loved God with his whole heart and had a kind word for everyone.

Buck will finally be inducted into the Baseball Hall of Fame in 2022. During the last mass induction of Negro League players in 2006, Buck was overlooked by the committee. He probably should have been disgusted and angry with the committee for their mistake, but that was not his way. When asked to speak on behalf of the many deceased inductees, Buck happily accepted. I am including part of his speech. It shows the true character of the man.

"And I tell you what, they always said to me, Buck. 'I know you hate people for what they did to you or what they did to your folks.' I said, 'No man, I never learned to hate.' I hate cancer. Cancer killed my mother. My wife died ten years ago of cancer. I hate AIDS. A good friend of mine died of AIDS three months ago. But I can't hate a human being, because my God never made anything ugly. Now you can be ugly if you want to be, boy, but God didn't make you that way. Uh, uh. So, I want you to light this valley up this afternoon. Martin (Luther King) said Agape (love) is understanding, creative, a redemptive good will toward all men. Agape is an overflowing love which seeks nothing in return. And when you reach love on this level, you love all men, not because you like them, not because their way appeals to you, but you love them because God loved them. And I love Jehovah my God with all my heart, with all my soul, and I love every one of you, as I love myself."

Buck was a man, who had every right to be bitter for being ignored by the Hall of Fame, but he responded with love. Thankfully, the veterans committee had righted that wrong and he will finally be enshrined where he belongs in the summer of 2022. If you are ever in Kansas City, consider stopping off in the Negro League Baseball Museum. The president of the museum is Bob Kendrick. He is a great person to follow on social media and an expert storyteller. He would testify to the heart of Buck O'Neil. He loved God and his fellow man with all his heart.

CHAPTER 3

ALL YOUR SOUL

So how do you love God with all your soul? The word soul has always been a difficult one to comprehend. The dictionary has several definitions including: the spiritual part of a person or the immortal part of a human that lives on past death. Hollywood and children's books have taught us that the soul floats away from your body when you die.

I think back to when I was first dating my lovely wife. We went to the theatre to watch a "chick flick" called "Ghost". Patrick Swayze's character dies early in the movie and his soul (or ghost) leaves his body. It floats around for the next hour trying to solve his murder and protect Demi Moore. If the word "ditto" just popped into your head, then you remember the movie. It makes us believe that our soul might just float around after our own death.

When I think about the idea of someone's soul, I believe it refers to the depth of a person. We might hear someone speaking and believe what they are saying on the surface but stop there. If we really believe something in our soul, then we are convinced and committed to it. We will not change our opinion easily or give up for anything. It's as if, our soul can hold onto something for us like an anchor. Thinking about it in those terms, loving God with all our soul means we are anchored into him. Our relationship with God is not based on some frivolous superficial love that we allow to change with the wind. It is a much deeper and permanent love. One that reflects commitment engrained into our thoughts and actions.

I began attending church as a teenager and had little previous experience with reading the Bible. One of the first scriptures that really grabbed ahold of me was Matthew 16:26. "What good will it be for a man if he gains the whole world, yet forfeits his soul? Or what can a man give in exchange for his soul?" Although we were far from wealthy growing up, I still had an appreciation for "stuff". This verse always reminded me that material possessions can consume us. God was reminding me to treasure my own soul over everything else. If God was so concerned about my soul, I should value it more that everything else. If we become obsessed with material wealth, status, or simply ourselves, we could neglect our own soul. God is telling us that our soul is our most valuable possession. Once we recognize that fact, loving God with all our soul is the best offering we can give to the Lord.

A great example of a man who believed in loving God with all his soul was William Booth. He founded the Christian Mission (later renamed the Salvation Army) in East London in 1865. He said that God had given him a love for the outcast and unloved of London. He had attended many of the popular churches of London but came away disappointed. He found that most of the churches only gave seats to the people who could pay for them. He was sure that was not the way that God had intended churches to behave. He was referred to as "the Prophet of the Poor" in his life story by Thomas Coates. It was a fitting nickname. He went far beyond just starting a church for the unwanted from the London streets. He went on to establish homes for the homeless, he opened a farm community (Hadleigh Farm) to train the urban poor, started a home for women, and worked with the prisoners and drunkards.

In the book "Booth the Beloved" by J. Evans Smith, Booth preached: "While women weep, as they do now, I'll fight; while little children go hungry, I'll fight; while men go to prison, in and out, in and out, as they do now, I'll fight; while there is a drunkard left, while there is a poor lost girl upon the streets, where there remains one dark soul without the light of God, I'll fight. I'll fight to the very end."

William Booth was well known for his philosophy of "Soup, soap and salvation". He said, "You cannot warm the hearts of people with God's love if they have an empty stomach and cold feet." He did not just preach at people. He loved on them by feeding them and clothing them first. He felt that once you had helped restore a person's dignity, then you could share your witness of God's love effectively. William Booth also encouraged women the share equally in ministry. His wife Catherine took over the leadership of the Salvation Army after his death. He was remembered as a man who knew how to love God with all his soul.

CHAPTER 4

ALL YOUR MIND

Loving God with all our mind might be the toughest of all. A few centuries ago, it probably was not this difficult. If you think back to the "Little House on the Prairie" show, life seemed simple. People would have more time to focus their minds on God. Today with everything at our fingertips, on our phones or on the many screens we see throughout the day, our minds are always being overwhelmed. We are constantly bombarding our minds with sounds, images, and distractions. The Ingalls family wouldn't have received instant updates on Facebook about their distant relative's vacation. Their work wouldn't have been sending them emails telling them that there was a problem with their current project.

It has become increasingly difficult to focus our minds on the Lord. Each step we take today, something else is trying to catch our attention. God wants our minds centered on him, so he can help guide our thoughts and actions. When we spend too much time thinking about ourselves and our devices, we sacrifice the time we should focus on loving others. Our thoughts take us in so many competing directions and away from God. When we keep the spotlight on ourselves all the time, we will miss the cues that God is sending our way. We can easily become self-centered or what we called it as kids, "stuck up".

One of my favorite scriptures, that I use to bring me down off my "high horse," when I start feeling this way, is Romans 12:1-3. "Therefore, I urge you, brothers, in view of God's mercy, to offer your bodies as living sacrifices, holy and pleasing to God- this is your spiritual act of worship. Do not conform any longer to the pattern of this world but be transformed by the renewing of your mind. Then you will be able to test and approve what God's will is- his good, pleasing and perfect will. For by the grace given me I say to every one of you: Do not think of yourself more highly than you ought, but rather think of yourself with sober judgement, in accordance with the measure of faith God has given you."

Sometimes, I find that I am focusing on myself too much, and that is easy to do when I spend all day walking alone on my mail route. When that happens, I try to remind myself that I am "thinking more highly of myself than I ought". God took his time creating us, so yes, we are all very special to him. He just wants to remind us that he created everyone else, and they are just as special to him. If we spend all our time and attention focused inward or on our devices, and less on God, we will miss how incredible the people around us really are. By keeping our minds centered on God, he will show us how to love our neighbors with his perfect love.

We can easily cause ourselves to be anxious and stressed out, when we focus inwardly. It is easy for us to become overwhelmed. We feel that there is too much happening, and we find that we simply can't keep up. Honestly, this happens to everyone at some point in their lives. Remember when we were children, and we were expected to memorize long lists of items. We felt like our brains would explode. Later, in high school and college we faced exam week the same way. I remember getting the exam schedule and finding out that I had three exams in a twenty-four-hour period. No sleep, lots of caffeine, and buckets of stress, but somehow, I pulled through. "Life was going to be so much easier when I got older." I would tell myself. I would only have to work forty-hours a week. No more going to college and working full-time. Can you picture those days? I would be able to come home from work and have every evening free to do anything we wanted with no obligations. I can't seem to remember it working out that way.

Once I graduated college, I couldn't find a teaching position, so I took a job at the post office. Like many of you, I soon found out that work took over my life. I would often have to work six days a week with lots of overtime. If I tried hard, I could scrape up some free time to relax or play. Then we had a baby! Anyone who had to work and raise a family knows where this is going. A few years ago, multitasking became a popular word. Working parents have been multitasking years before it was a fad.

With all of this going on, life can quickly start crushing us under its weight. We can become exhausted physically or worse, emotionally. David asked God in Psalms 139:23 to "Search me, O God, and know my heart; test me and know my anxious thoughts." God understands that life has a way of steamrolling over us, if we let it. How can we deal with all of it? Unfortunately, many people don't. They check out. They turn to drugs, alcohol, or something else to stop or postpone the pain.

Paul tells us in Philippians 4:6 "Do not be anxious about anything, but in everything, by prayer and petition, with thanksgiving, present your requests to God." I know that sounds a little too easy. If we get stressed out, just pray and it will all go away. It's probably not going to be that simple. Our problems will still be there, but maybe by slowing down and trusting God to help, we can see a clearer way through. Set your mind on Christ and take things one step at a time. You couldn't study for all three exams at the same time. And you'll find that you can't solve all your problems by wishing them away or ignoring them. Faith in God, and a calmer mindset will help you through the situation. It will get easier. Take that from a guy who is looking towards retirement in a few years. God is telling us to keep our thoughts and our minds anchored in him, and he will help us carry our burdens.

When I think of role models from my life and studies that carried heavy burdens, two more baseball players come to mind, Jackie Robinson and Hank Aaron. You have probably figured out that baseball is my favorite sport. As a child, I dreamed of playing in the Major Leagues, but life and my talent level took me in a different direction. Most Americans are quite aware of the story of Jackie Robinson. He carried the burden of an entire race unto the field of baseball. He faced hatred everywhere he went but kept his mind focused and did not allow hate to sidetrack him from his mission. If you don't know his story, put a bookmark in this book and go watch the movie 42; I'll wait.

Hank Aaron faced many of the same challenges that Jackie Robinson battled through. He might not have been the first black player to break the color barrier in baseball, but he was close behind. He fought the same fight, trying to earn respect and decent treatment. He was subject to the same hatred and discrimination that all black players were facing, trying to play the game they loved.

Every year on the anniversary of Hank Aaron breaking Babe Ruth's historic home run record, I listen to the broadcast of the at bat by the legendary announcer Vin Scully. After Aaron hit the record-breaking home run, Scully lets the radio listener hear the crowd cheering and the fireworks exploding, then he says: "What a marvelous moment for baseball, what a marvelous moment for Atlanta and the state of Georgia. What a marvelous moment for the country and the world. A black man is getting a standing ovation in the deep south for breaking the record of an all-time baseball idol and it is a great moment for all of us and particularly for Henry Aaron."

Until recently, I thought just as it appears Vin Scully had thought. Racism must have ended right there, because everyone was cheering for Aaron. It sounded perfect coming from probably the most beloved baseball announcer of all time. The south had clearly accepted Aaron even though he was black. In 2021, days after Henry Aaron's death, Bob Kendrick (President of the Negro League Hall of Fame) explained the true reality of the event on Buster Olney's Baseball Tonight podcast. "Those death threats he was getting were very real, particularly in his mind and in his heart, because you have to realize that he had witnessed in his time, the assassination of Dr. Martin Luther King Jr., the assassination of John F. Kennedy, the assassination of Malcolm X. So, there are no hollow threats for a black man in the deep south, so you had to take this stuff real and the weight of this." He added that, "twenty-seven years after Jackie Robison breaking the color barrier, Aaron was still subjected to the same level of hate and vitriol that we saw with Jackie Robinson. And both men handled it with such grace and class and dignity. Aaron never harbored any ill will or bitterness."

A few days after Aaron's death in January 2021, Bob Kendrick was also quoted in USA Today. "I'm glad that he (Aaron) lived long enough that he could relish what he was able to do. And I think people became more accepting and appreciative of that, through the years. He was a special human being." When I think of Hank Aaron, I see a man who kept his mind centered on God. He was battered constantly with hate mail, death threats, and anger but he did not allow it to change where his mind was centered.

My last thoughts on loving God with all your mind deal with my own life experiences. I have always considered myself to be intelligent. I figured that I knew what was best for my life and dismissed the opinions of others. I felt like I could weigh the pros and cons of any decision and choose the right, intelligent option. Now I'm sure that I am not the only person who thought he knew the best plan for his own life. It's not like I was saying "get out of my way God, I know what's best for my life," but maybe I was.

I can give you a crazy example from my college years. I was working at a movie theatre in 1987, when the movie "The Million Dollar Mystery" was released. As a promotion for the movie, the studio left a puzzle for the audience to solve. If you solved the mystery and found the location of the hidden money, then you would win a million dollars. Well Mr. Smarty Pants Jim Bethel obviously figured out the answer. The money was hidden in the bridge of the nose of the Statue of Liberty. I submitted my entry and began making my plans for the money. Over the next few weeks, I found myself making deals with God during my prayers. I had it all figured out. This money would solve all my problems. It would pay for college and still leave me plenty left over to do good things for God. I knew what was best for me and I let it consume my thoughts and prayers. Finally, I found out that thousands of people solved the riddle, and they had a drawing to pick a winner, surprise it wasn't me.

I had taken my focus off God and was making all my plans for my future on my own. God was trying to show me that I needed to trust myself less and him more. When I remembered to love God with all my mind, life came back into focus. If we let him direct our mind, our thoughts won't be solely on ourselves. Once we make the change, God will show us how to love others with his perfect unselfish love.

CHAPTER 5

ALL YOUR STRENGTH

I know, loving God with all your strength sounds exhausting. If I use all my strength to love God, how will I have enough left over to survive day to day? This sounds rather corny, but God will provide you with the strength to move forward. The most obvious Bible quote I can throw out here is Philippians 4:13. "I can do all things through Christ who strengthens me."

So, does this mean that God wants me to use every ounce of energy in my body to love him? He does, but not exclusively in the way we think. By serving others, we are serving him. By loving others, we are loving him. By standing up for others, we are standing up for him. When we see others in need, and reach out a hand to help, we are using our strength for the Lord. When we love our neighbor, we are showing God's love.

When my son graduated college and was moving to New York City, I wrote him a letter of fatherly advice. In it I reminded him that we have four major resources in our life that are limited. They are our time, money, focus, and energy. These resources are dependent on each other. To gain more of one means we must sacrifice one or more of the others. Life must be a balance of these choices. For example, if you decide you want to make more money, you might have to work longer hours. This decision will steal from your other resources of time and energy, and maybe even your focus. When God tells us to love him with all our heart, soul, mind, and strength, he is cognizant of this delicate balance.

From time to time, we will find that our energy or strength

is running dangerously low. When this happens, some will turn to drugs, caffeine, or energy drinks. I believe that God wants us to turn to him for help. Paul writes in 2 Corinthians 12:10, "For when I am weak, then I am strong." Wait, what? He is trying to say, that once he realizes that he has run out of his own strength and remembers to allow God to provide for him, then he has unlimited strength. Once we stop counting on ourselves for everything and lean into God's love, then we will become strong.

I can think of countless examples of individuals or groups that serve the Lord with all their strength. Missionaries all around the world have given up comfortable lives to serve others. They serve God with all their strength by serving others. Many people work tirelessly in homeless shelters and soup kitchens providing for the needy in just about every major city in the world. There are thousands of doctors, nurses, and dentists who travel overseas or into underserved neighborhoods to help others. My own dentist, Patrick Daulton, travels to Central America often to offer his services to others.

There may be no better example of someone who loved God with all her strength then Mother Theresa. For her, serving others was the greatest way she could love God. She always put the comfort of others before her own personal comfort. She won the Noble Peace Prize in 1979. She started her acceptance speech by offering a prayer by St. Francis of Assisi.

"Lord make me a channel of your peace, that where there is hatred, I may bring love; that where there is wrong, I may bring the spirit of forgiveness; that where there is discord, I may bring harmony; that where there is error, I may bring truth; that where there is doubt, I may bring faith; that where there is despair, I may bring hope; that where there are shadows, I may bring light; that where there is sadness, I may bring you. Lord, grant that I may seek rather to comfort than to be comforted; to understand, than to be understood; to love, than to be loved. For it is by forgetting self, that one finds. It is by forgiving that one is forgiven. It is by dying, that one awakens to eternal life, amen."

She revealed the story of her life with this prayer. Her whole life was dedicated to serving God by serving others. She used all her strength and more to show a dying world, God's love. She spent her life putting others before herself. She was more concerned about comforting others than living a comfortable life. She stressed understanding and loving others over being understood or loved.

Later in her speech she gave a great example of someone loving their neighbor. "One evening a gentleman came to our house and spoke. 'There is a Hindu family, and their eight children have not eaten for a long time. Do something for them.' And I took rice, and I went immediately and there was this mother, those little faces. Shining eyes from sheer hunger. She took the rice from my hand, she divided it into two and went out. When she came back, I asked her, 'Where did you go? What did you do?' And one answer she gave me. 'They are hungry also.' She knew that the next-door neighbor, a Muslim family was hungry. What surprised me most, not that she gave the rice, but what surprised me most, that in her suffering, in her hunger, she knew that somebody else was hungry, and she had the courage to share, share the love."

In Mother Theresa's example, the neighbor actually lived next-door. That was how we defined the term neighbor when we were toddlers. In truth, in our modern world, everyone is our neighbor. Our next-door neighbor might be in need, but so might someone we see on the street or at the store. Mother Theresa is asking us to open our hearts that we might see the needs of others, instead of focusing all our strength on our own needs. I understand what it is like to work too many hours or be pulled in ten different directions at once. God is reminding us that he has plenty of strength to share with us. He asks that we look around and see a hurting world that needs our love and help.

I found a list of Mother Theresa's famous quotes and would like to share a few.

"Spread love everywhere you go. Let no one ever come to

you without leaving happier."

"Not all of us can do great things. But we can do small things with great love."

"If you can't feed a hundred people, then feed just one."

"If you judge people, you have no time to love them."

"God doesn't require that you succeed, he only requires that you try."

The one that really weighs on me is her quote about judging others. I feel like we all (including me) spend too much time judging others. We blame them for the circumstances they are in. We decide that we don't have to help them since they created their own problem. We spend all our own time and energy blaming our neighbor for their situation instead of offering a helping hand. Here's the truth. God did not give us the right to judge others, that's his job. We are wasting our strength trying to do God's job and neglecting our own. We are here to love God and love others period. Many of us know John 3:16 but forget verse 17. "For God did not send his Son into the world to condemn the world, but to save the world through him." If Jesus wasn't expected to condemn others, why do we spend so much time taking that job on ourselves. Mother Theresa was showing us how to love God with all her strength, by loving others and expecting nothing in return. She is a perfect example for us to follow.

CHAPTER 6

WHO IS MY NEIGHBOR?

Alright, so here come the tricky question. Who is my neigh-bor? It sounds like the title of a Dr. Seuss book. When I was young, I would have told you the people on my street were my neigh-bors. If I could see your house from my front door, then you were my neighbor. Then television started changing things for me. I watched Sesame Street and Mr. Rogers and started feeling like I had neighbors that I simply hadn't met yet. As I grew older, my neighborhood grew exponentially. Once I got a bike, the whole development was filled with my neighbors. Eventually, I got a car and now the whole city became my neighborhood. Now with the internet and cell phones, the whole world is my neighborhood.

In August 1963, Dr. King gave his "I have a dream" speech. He hoped that everyone who heard it would expand their vision of neighbors. He started by saying, "I have a dream that one day on the red hills of Georgia, the sons of former slaves and the sons of former slave owners will be able to sit down together at the table of brotherhood." He was painting a picture where color and family history would not matter. We would be able to enjoy a meal together with our neighbors and ignore our pasts. Later in the speech King added, "One day right down in Alabama. Little black boys and black girls will be able to join hands with little white boys and white girls as sisters and brothers."

I remember hearing a little about Dr. King's "I have a dream speech" in school. I had no idea of the lengths that some groups of people were going to, to keep the races apart. I had also heard of the "Brown vs Board of Education" case from 1954. It basically said that separating children in public schools by race was unconstitutional. I knew that busing and school integration were touchy subjects with some of my relatives but didn't understand why. My high school history teachers always ran out of time in the school year, so we breezed right past the Civil Rights movement. Years later, I was shocked to learn that in reaction to the "Brown vs Board of Education" ruling several school districts simply closed their schools instead of integrating.

Let that sink in for a minute, if you were as uneducated as I was on the subject. While Dr. King was making his speech, Prince Edward County in Virginia (a three-hour drive from Washington D.C.) was continuing to have its public schools closed for five years. The leaders of the county and the school district were so opposed to letting whites and blacks in the same schools that they closed all their public schools. Dr. King was trying hard to tell them to just "Love Their Neighbor".

Very few of us know these stories. Why? Did we have bad history teachers or was teaching about Civil Rights not part of the "approved curriculum"? I cannot be certain, but I would hazard to guess that most history books from the 20th century were written by white men. They might have been instructed to make all American history look rosy and kind. They were willing to overlook or ignore Civil Rights violations from our own history. So, unless you were part of the fight for equality in education and life in general, you probably haven't heard these stories. I know that "hindsight is 20/20" but looking back at incidents like the integration of the "Little Rock Nine" makes me sick to my stomach. The idea that hundreds of white families were screaming hateful words and threats at nine black children, who simply wanted to get a quality education is shameful still today. I know that mobs can cause people to do and say things they normally wouldn't, but if you were outside of that school in Little Rock, I hope you feel ashamed looking back. The fact is, several states including Arkansas and Virginia decided to suspend the laws in their states that require compulsory education. They did this so they could close public schools to keep whites and blacks from mixing. These actions are a scar on our country's history and need to be told. I bring this history up to remind us, that even though Christ told us almost 2000 years ago to love our neighbor, we still have a lot of work to do.

Eleven years before Dr. King's speech, Dr. Billy Graham had similar run-ins with racism. According to writings in the Billy Graham Library, Graham was scheduled to hold a crusade in Jackson, Mississippi. "Ropes were erected to keep blacks and whites apart, When Graham arrived at the meeting, he actually physically took the ropes down and symbolically, in doing so, said, 'Look we're all equal before God, we're all one together and every man has his right, for the rights that we enjoy and want'." I'm sure by doing this, he made many southerners angry. They might have left out of anger. Graham knew that he was following Christ's teachings. He was reminding everyone in attendance to "Love their neighbor".

Christianity Today published part of a message he preached on October 4, 1993. In this message on racism, he stated: "We must not underestimate the devastating effects of racism on our world. Daily headlines chronicle its grim toll: divide nations and families, devastating wars and human suffering on an unimaginable scale, a constant downward spiral of poverty and hopelessness, children broken in body and warped in mind... Racial and ethnic hatred is a sin, and we need to label it as such. Jesus told his disciples to 'love their neighbor as yourself'. Racism is a sin precisely because it keeps us from obeying God's command to love our neighbors."

CHAPTER 7

UNCONDITIONAL LOVE

In Matthew 5:43-47, Jesus tells his followers, "You have heard that it was said 'Love your neighbor and hate your enemy'. But I tell you: Love your enemies and pray for those who persecute you, that you may be sons of you Father in heaven. He causes his sun to rise on the evil and the good and sends rain on the righteous and unrighteous. If you love those who love you, what reward will you get? Are not even the tax collectors doing that? And if you greet only your brothers, what are you doing more than others? Do not even the pagans do that?"

Christ was saying to the people, "Wake up! We can't go around hating people who are different than us." He is reminding us that anyone can love the people that love them back. He is calling us to be better than that. We find it so easy to put conditions on our love. "If you do things for me and make me happy, then I will love you." That's not how God planned things. He wants us to follow the example that Christ set for us. He wants us to love unconditionally.

Think back to the vows you heard at any traditional wedding that you have attended. I know that I promised my wife to love her "for better, for worse, for richer, for poorer, in sickness and in health, to love and to cherish, till death do us part." Nowhere in my vows did I say, "but only if you do the same for me". I promised to hold up my end of the vow, regardless of what she did for me. That's what unconditional love means. There are no restrictions or limits, no list of things I need in return for my love.

I promised to love her to the end. That's the same love Christ has for us. He wants us to follow his example.

I have a dog on my mail route that understands uncondi-tional love (most dogs do). Sophie is an English Cream Golden Re-triever. If she sees me on the route, she'll head right to me. When she gets next to me, she leans into me as a sign of love and trust. She normally sheds copious amounts of white fur wherever she goes. Oftentimes in the winter, I'll notice white fur on my black gloves. Even if I haven't seen Sophie for weeks, I know its her love rubbing off on me. She was just leaving some of her unconditional love with me to take along on a long day. We need to be like Sophie and leave traces of ourselves on the people we encounter every day. Hopefully, the trace we leave will be of love and acceptance, not anger or hate.

Later in Matthew 25: 35-36, Jesus tells the parable of the sheep and goats. "For I was hungry, and you gave me something to eat, I was thirsty, and you gave me something to drink, I was a stranger, and you invited me in, I needed clothes, and you clothed me, I was sick, and you looked after me, I was in prison, and you came to visit me." They were confused and asked when this had happened? Jesus said, "I tell you the truth, whatever you did for one of the least of these brothers of mine, you did for me."

Christ was reminding his followers that when they provide for their neighbors, they are serving him. He was prompting them to seek out opportunities to show love to those who need it most. One of the best examples, in our history, of people who sought opportunities to serve others in need, would be the Underground Railroad. There were hundreds of men, women, and families who sacrificed their resources, time, and homes to help secret runaway slaves to freedom. They mostly operated under the cover of night, helping conduct their unknown neighbors northward to non-slave states. There are many compelling stories and countless arti-facts available for viewing at the National Underground Railroad Freedom Center in Cincinnati, Ohio. The conductors who served along the Underground Railroad understood Christ's call for us to provide for our brothers and sisters. "I tell you the truth, whatever you did for one of the least of these brothers of mine, you did for me."

In John 15:9-13, Jesus advises us. "As the Father has loved me, so have I loved you. Now remain in my love. If you obey my commands, you will remain in my love, just as I have obeyed my Father's commands and remain in his love. I have told you this so that my joy may be in you and that your joy may be complete. My command is this: Love each other as I have loved you. Greater love has no one than this, that he lay down his life for his friend."

Many families faced this situation (or opportunity) during the World War II. The Germans were rounding up Jewish people for imprisonment and extermination. In 1941, the Germans issued the Third Decree of the General Governor. It said that if Jews left their designated residential areas (prison camps), they would be punished with death. It also said that the same penalty would be applied to anyone who provided refuge to Jews. Most of us probably read "The Diary of Anne Frank" as children or can remember her story. Thousands of Jews were hiding throughout Europe for years to escape certain death during the holocaust. The people who took great risks, placing their own families in danger to hide Jews, were living a life of loving their neighbor.

While researching this book, I came across a story of a Nazi officer who claimed he never took part in the holocaust. He visited the death camps but left without participating in executions. As bad as it sounds, many of us have done something similar. This officer might have been able to help some of the Jews or perhaps stopped some of the torture, but he chose to walk away. Have we been in a situation where we could help a neighbor in need, but chose to walk away? It says in James 4:17: "Anyone, then, who knows the good he ought to do and doesn't do it, sins." If we can help our neighbor, then we should feel an obligation to do so. People who are living a life of loving their neighbor, don't walk away.

We've come a long way as a civilization from slavery and genocide. I would hope that now most of us would stand up for the nine children integrating in Little Rock High School. I expect that we would lead a public outcry, if school leaders tried to close schools to block anyone from attending school freely. And if any race of people decided to try and exterminate another, we would stand in the way. We have come a long way, but the journey to "loving you neighbor" regardless of their skin color or religious beliefs, still has a way to go. As Paul says in Galatians 6:9, "Let us not become weary in doing good."

CHAPTER 8
Taking a Risk to Help Your Neighbor

Anyone who attended Sunday school as a child or knows their Bible was wondering when I would bring up the "Parable of the Good Samaritan". If you don't know the story here is a quick synopsis: A Jewish man was traveling from Jerusalem to Jericho, he got mugged and beaten half to death. A priest saw him and passed by without helping. A Levite (probably a priest assistant or leader at a local synagogue) passed by without helping either. Then a Samaritan (the enemy of the Jew) stopped to help him. He then took the beaten man to a local inn and paid for his further care.

When I heard messages on the parable, we always ridiculed the priest and Levite for their unwillingness to help care for one of their flock. We never mention that the road they were traveling on was referred to as the "Bloody Pass". It was a very curvy trail that was known for criminal activity. If the priest or Levite would have stopped to help, they would have put themselves at risk. Which makes the Samaritan's gesture even more noble. The other two men had not heard the "Parable of the Sheep and Goats". They would possibly ask, "Lord, when did we see you hungry or thirsty or a stranger or needing clothes or sick or in prison, and not help you?"

Whether it was fate or not, the last message that Dr. Martin Luther King Jr. preached the night before his assassination was called, "The Goodness of the Good Samaritan". In his sermon, Dr. King praised the Samaritan's ability to look beyond "accidents of race, religion and nationality". He was reminding us that when God sees us, he doesn't see our skin color or what language our Bible is printed in, he sees our heart. Dr. King pleaded with his audience. "Something must happen so to touch the hearts and souls of men that they will come together because it is natural and right." Before he finished, he encouraged his listeners to "Go out with the conviction that all men are brothers, tied in a single garment of destiny."

He gave his own definition of who your neighbor really is. "He is anyone to whom you prove to be neighborly. He is anyone lying in need on life's roadside." Meaning that anyone we can help, is our neighbor. If someone is starving ten thousand miles away, and we can help them, then they are our neighbor. He added that, "One of the great tragedies of man's long trek up the highway of history has been his all to prevalent tendency to limit his neighborly concern to the race, the tribe, the class or the nation." King reminded us all. "The ultimate measure of a man is not where he stands in moments of comfort and moments of convenience, but where he stands in moments of challenge and moments of controversy. The true neighbor is the man who will risk his position, his prestige and even his life for the welfare of others."

We may find at times that loving our neighbor might make us uncomfortable or even unpopular with our family. Maybe we can win them over to our side by setting an example like "The Good Samaritan" did. We simply cannot continue living a life of crossing the street to put distance between ourselves and a neighbor in need. We need to reach out a hand and not walk away from them.

CHAPTER 9

WELCOME YOUR NEIGHBORS

How should we show love to our neighbors? Some of the best verses in the Bible that speak about love come from the "Love chapter", 1st Corinthians 13. Many ministers utilize this scripture as part of their marriage ceremonies. The minister encourages the newly married couple to try and live a married life that follows the "Love chapter". I want to stress verses 4 to 8. "Love is patient, love is kind. It does not envy, it does not boast, it is not proud. It is not rude, it is not self-seeking, it is not easily angered, it keeps no record of wrongs. Love does not delight in evil but rejoices with the truth. It always protects, always trusts, always hopes, always perseveres. Love never fails."

I know this scripture is a lot. It basically sounds like we need to be perfect. I have been married to my lovely wife for more than thirty years and have fallen short of these verses many times. God knows we aren't going to pull this off perfectly. He understands that we will fail at times. He just wants our best effort. He reminds us in Romans 5:8. "But God demonstrates his own love for us in this: While we were still sinners, Christ died for us." He 's not waiting for us to have this perfect love nailed down, he loves us where we are in life.

Looking back at the "Love chapter", how can we apply this to loving our neighbor? Well to start with we could try to be a little more patient and kinder. It is amazing how we expect others to be perfect even though we are all far from it. Your neighbors and friends aren't perfect, and that's okay. They are going to mess up and we need to be patient with them, just as we hope they will be patient with us. We need to try and overlook their shortcomings and see them as people full of potential like us. Emerson had a quote I like: "Treat a man as he is, and he will remain as he is. Treat a man as he could be, and he will become what he should be." Meaning that if we believe that our friends and neighbor have great potential, then we should treat them that way.

The verses from 1st Corinthians remind us not to be boastful or proud, rude or self-seeking. As hard as it may be sometimes, we need to avoid reacting in anger. I agree that patience and understanding are extremely difficult skills to acquire. I have found personally, with age, that I have learned to be somewhat more patient, but I know that I have plenty more work to do in this area. The verse "keeps no record of wrongs" tends to get rushed over. It may be the most important part of a successful marriage and it's probably the same for good friendships and being a good neighbor. God is basically telling us that we need to become more forgetful. We can all admit that it's easy to forget where we left the car keys, but not easy to forget what someone said about us. We like to hold tight to our grudges and bad memories. God is willing to forgive our atrocious behaviors and sins; he is reminding us that we need to do the same or our neighbors. We need to be willing to give them the same clean slate that God gives us.

If we believe that love should "always protect, always trust, always hope, always persevere", then we should show that in our everyday actions. We should hope for the best for others. Too often we think that in life, for us to succeed others must fail. Life is not really a game of Jenga. I shouldn't be cheering for someone else to knock over life's tower of blocks, so I will be declared the winner. How many lives could we impact for the good, if we expressed this kind of love for our neighbors? Suicide is one of the leading causes of death in our world. The statistics I read were breath-takingly bad. I remember the movies they showed us in school health class. The victims were often crying out for help, but no one seemed to hear them. If we spent more time loving our neighbors, instead of beating them at the game of life, we would probably become better at hearing their cries for help. Our own hearts and mind would become more in tune, and we would recognize when others are in need. We might even learn to take the time to actually listen to our neighbors. The next time we ask: "How are you doing?", let's listen for a response and not use it as a throw away line of greeting. If we stop and really hear their response, we might find out that things aren't "fine", then we can take the time to help them.

Over my thirty years of delivering mail, I've been on a lot of front porches. I've seen a vast collection of door mats that have caught my attention. Some are funny like "Hope you brought pizza" or "Friends are always welcome, Family by appointment only". I've even seen one that made me hope it was meant to be funny "Come back with a warrant". But I did a double take the other day when I saw one that read "Yay, You're Here". I thought, "Wouldn't it be nice if that's how we felt when we met everyone." Every time someone showed up at our house or in our life, we were truly excited to see them.   In our neighborhood, almost everyone has a wooden sign on their front porch that reads "Welcome" or "Home", "Family" or "Ohio State". Are we really telling people they are welcome or even wanted at our house or in our lives? When we were selling our house a few years back, we borrowed our neighbor's "Welcome" sign for our open house. After we moved, we came home one day to find a new "Home" sign waiting for us. Our old neighbors wanted us to know that even though we lived fifteen miles away, we were still neighbors. ("Thanks Dave and Sandy.") We should all strive to live life the way our sign or doormats say: Our homes and lives are open to our friends and neighbors.

If we want to show love to our neighbors, it all starts with our attitude. I heard a piece of advice that I am trying to put into action in my own life. The speaker said that the best way to change your attitude on anything is to change how you think about it. Instead of saying "I have to" say "I get to". It changes the thing from a chore to an opportunity. I have to go to work is a depressing phrase. I get to go to work reminds me that we have a job to provide for our families. I have to mow the grass is a chore. I get to mow the grass means I own a house and have achieved one of my dreams. Of course, this doesn't work all the time. I get to shovel two feet of snow is still a tough pill to swallow. But it will change our attitude about a lot of the activities we do day after day.

Daisy Bates is a great example of someone who opened her life and home to her neighbors. Her home became the makeshift headquarters for the fight to integrate Central High School in Little Rock in 1957. I previously mentioned the battles the "Little Rock Nine" faced when they tried to attend the segregated high school. Daisy Bates served on the front line helping the children and supporting their families. She was subjected to continual threats and harassment from her community.

Daisy and her husband published a weekly African American newspaper called the "Arkansas State Press". The paper inspired many during the Civil Rights movement. During the integration of Central High School, Daisy was confronted by the Christian Women's Club of Little Rock. They advised Daisy to withdraw her support for "the Little Rock Nine" or face the consequences. She refused to abandon the movement and suffered for her decision. The Christian Women's Club leaned on all her advertisers and caused them to withdraw their business with the newspaper. As a result, the "Arkansas State Press" went out of business.

As a Christian myself, it is painful to think that a group using Christ's name in their title, would act in such a way. Did they really think that Christ would condone discrimination? For hundreds of years, people who called themselves Christians acted that way. Once again, I can hear the verse "Love your neighbor as yourself" in my head. Daisy Bates had opened her home and life to show love and support her neighbors. That is a true example of "loving your neighbor". The Christian Women's Club's response was like what we see everywhere today. If we hear or see something that we don't agree with, we try to get them cancelled. Remember what Mother Theresa said: "If you judge people, you have no time to love them". Christ wants us to stand up for others in his name. Christ wants us to love others in his name. He'll take care of any judging that needs to be done.

CHAPTER 10

IT'S A MATTER OF PERSPECTIVE

When we look back at history, we are amazed at some of the dumb things we did. We have progressed over time but still have a way to go. Showing love to your neighbor is an ever-evolving life choice. When we look back at decisions we have made as humans, the phrase that comes to mind is: "How could we be so stupid?". Enslaving others to do our labor, closing schools to keep races separated, or letting a dictator round up people from different ethnic groups for extermination are things we would now consider uncivilized.

Reading as much as I do and studying history, I take the concept of "walking a mile in someone else's shoes" seriously. It has helped me understand groups like BLM a little better. None of us are truly free until everyone is free from suppression. When I was student-teaching, I taught a lesson on perspective consciousness. My goal was to try and teach the students that there are different viewpoints. We need to try and see events from another perspective to gain a better understanding of history. I split the class in half and assigned separate readings to the two groups. The story was about Stanley and Livingstone's encounter with natives in the Congo. Although both stories were about the same event, they were from different viewpoints. One was from Stanley and the other was from the natives. We discussed both stories in class. Eventually, I had to explain that it was the same story, just from different viewpoints.

I was tying to show the class that the history we read in books or the newspaper, or the television newscast is presented from someone's perspective. We should try to hear multiple sides of the story before accepting it as fact. I'm sure that German school children were not supplied with the facts of the holocaust. Just as American children were not always given the truths of the Civil Rights movement. Still today, or maybe especially today, we are not given all the facts by the media or politicians. They want everything to fit their particular narrative. They purposely want to make it difficult to find out the truth, so we will remain divided. When we are a divided people, it is harder to "love your neighbor".

We need to reach out to others and take the time to listen to their side. We should learn their perspective and try to understand them before shoving our opinions in their face. We should be willing to listen and accept others because Christ showed us the same love and understanding. It is not a job or obligation; it is an opportunity to do better today than yesterday.

One of the phrases that I remember from European History class was "noblesse obliges". Webster defines it as: "The obligation of honorable, generous, and responsible behavior associated with high role or birth". From my studies at Ohio State, I learned a more cynical definition. It was the way that European nobles felt they had to show pity on serfs and servants. They would provide a minimum standard of living for the workers and by doing this, it showed how great and generous they were. God doesn't want us to love our neighbors because it makes us look better or more royal. He doesn't expect us to pat ourselves on the back for our own generosity. He wants us to do it because it's best for everyone and it reflects the love that he has shown us.

It's hard for us to remember that everyone you meet in life was raised differently than you. We all truly come from different backgrounds. The person you run into at the local McDonalds may come from a divorced family and never had a male or female role model in their life. We are all quick to assume and judge, based on our own standards and life situation. We may find it hard to trust others due to our upbringing. We may be naïve to others' problems or difficulties because we were sheltered. The point is, we all need to take a few extra minutes from our busy lives to try and understand where the other person is coming from.

During my second year of working at summer camp, I learned a lesson of my own about perspective. I had been promoted to program director and was responsible for most of the day-to-day operations involving the campers. The inner-city children from Columbus arrived early on Monday to begin their week at camp. Most of my counselors were teenagers and new to working with kids. By noon Tuesday, I realized that one of my counselors was on the edge of breaking down. One of his eight-year-old campers was driving him crazy. I knew that I had a decision to make. Send the child home or possibly lose a counselor. With encouragement from the camp caretaker, I decided to try a third option. I chose to adopt the camper as my new assistant for the rest of the week. He went with me everywhere. He slept on a mattress on the floor in my room. He woke up with me, made rounds with me, and took breaks with me. Wherever I went throughout the day, he was by my side. I tried to involve him in my decisions and actions to keep him busy and distracted. It was an exhausting week for me and probably for him as well, but we made it through. When the weekend finally arrived, I was glad to head home for some rest.

Sometime during the next week, the Salvation Army officer called me in to her office. She told me that she had just received a call from the young man's case officer. He had told his counselor that he had just had the best week of his life. I walked out of the office with a smile on my face and in my heart. I don't know if I really made a change in the boy's life, but he changed mine. I had been reminded that people don't need our judgement, they need our attention and love. This young man had been told he was a "bad kid" his whole life, he just wanted someone to believe in him and give him a chance. Although I never saw him again, he will always be my neighbor. He reminded me that we all come from different backgrounds and have different perspectives.

I got another lesson in perspective while I was coaching my son's third grade soccer travel team. We had traveled 100 miles south to play in a tournament in Cincinnati. On Friday night, I had to attend a coaches' meeting before the tournament started. The tournament director gave us an information packet. He pointed out that it included three "player of the match" medals. We were expected to award a medal after every match to a player on the opposing team. We could base it on skill or sportsmanship, our choice.

My son's team consisted of nine players with varying levels of skill and talent. They were considered the junior team for their age group. In a few years they would merge with the senior team, when the number of players and the size of the pitch increased. One of our newest players to the game was an African American kid named Bakari. We all called him Baks. He was a big kid, by soccer standards (he later switched to football). Since he was new to soccer, he was not as skilled as the other players. He always gave us his best effort and that was all I ever asked from a player. Everyone liked him and it was a privilege to coach him.

After the first match of the tournament on Saturday morning, I presented my medal to the best defender on the opposing team. The other coach gave his "player of the match" medal to Baks. We made our presentations in front of both teams for effect. The kids were excited from the game, and we left the pitch together as a rowdy team. We headed to a local restaurant to share lunch with the team. Later that afternoon, we played our second match. After it was over, I awarded my medal to the best offensive player from the other team. The other coach gave his medal to Baks.

Now I knew that Baks wasn't the "player of the match" in either game. It was not my place to say anything about the selection, so I patted him on the back and headed for the minivan. Once we were on the road and headed for the hotel, my nine-year-old had held his piece long enough. "Dad, why did both those coaches give the MVP medal to Baks? He isn't our best player."

Alright, quick parent test. What do I do here? I wasn't sure how to answer him. I didn't know what the other coaches were thinking. Do I tell my son that the other coaches felt guilty because Baks was the only black plyer on the pitch? Maybe they were just trying to encourage him to continue playing. He might have been easy to remember because of his skin color. I didn't want to speculate on any of the possibilities in the ten seconds I had to answer his question. I wanted to answer in terms he would understand. As far as I could remember, we had never treated anyone differently based on their skin color in front of our children. I didn't think that he thought that Baks was receiving the medal based on his skin color. I tried to explain that Baks had played as hard as everyone else. Since his skills weren't as polished as his teammates, it looked like he was working harder than them. The answer seemed to be sufficient because he dropped the subject.

On Sunday morning, we were playing our third and final match of the tournament. During warmups, the opposing coach approached me with a proposition. He asked if we could pick our own medal winner for the final game. I would have never proposed the idea, but I was happy that he had. When the match was over, I awarded the medal to the player he suggested. Here's the part that no one else knows, but I'm coming clean now. I told the coach to give his "player of the match" medal to my son. He was the best player on the team (I know every dad thinks that). He deserved it for having to deal with everything that comes up when you're the coach's kid. I was also relieved that I would not have to explain a third medal awarded to Baks.

I haven't seen Baks in several years, but I hope he treasured those medals. My own son has since moved on from college and now lives in New York City. He still has a room in our house that is filled with trophies and medals. I'm sure if I searched through it, I would find that medal. I know today that there are many heated discussions over equity and equality. I have always believed in treating everyone as equals because we were all created as equals by God. Sometimes it may be hard to do, but if we try to look at things from another's person's perspective, we might be a little more accepting of them.

CHAPTER 11
OFFERING GRACE AND PAYING IT FORWARD

One of the best ways we can show love to our neighbors and God is by offering them grace. We could prevent most of life's conflicts by offering grace to the person that offended us. What does it mean to offer someone grace? It basically means showing someone kindness when they don't deserve it. We can respond with kindness when they expect an argument or fight. Most of all, we forgive someone who hasn't asked for forgiveness. Now that's a hard one, isn't it? We were always taught as kids to say we were sorry. Offering grace means we are willing to forgive someone who didn't say they were sorry. It is an extremely challenging thing to do for all of us, including this "not so perfect" author.

When defining the term grace, my father-in-law used to say it was "the unmerited favor of God". We did nothing to deserve this grace from God, but he gave it to us freely out of his love for us. Jesus Christ is the finest example of someone who was willing to offer grace. He lived a sinless life but was willing to take on the cross and suffer for our sins. By dying this excruciatingly painful death, he covered the sins of hundreds of future generations. His gift of his own life was the ultimate offer of grace.

We should be willing to offer some of that grace to others in our daily life. Especially in truly meaningless matters. When someone cuts us off in traffic, we almost all get mad and want revenge. Why? Does it really matter? We need to offer them grace and just go on with our day. Life is not about getting even with everyone who upsets you. It is about coexisting on this small planet with everyone around us. The best way to do that is to offer grace to people who offend you.

A good example of someone who learned to offer grace in her life was Corrie ten Boom. She was a Christian working in the Netherlands during World War II. She tells her story in her book "The Hiding Place". During the holocaust, her family helped hide Jews from the Germans. They helped smuggle hundreds of Jews to freedom. They were finally caught by the German secret police in 1944. They were all sent to prison camps. Corrie and her sister were sent to Ravensbruck concentration camp. Life was very hard for them there. He sister died there after many torturous days. Corrie was only released due to a clerical error.

In 1947, Corrie was giving a lecture in Germany. Afterwards, she was approached by a man she recognized. He was a guard from the concentration camp who had tormented her and her sister. He thrust his hand out to thank her for the message she had shared. She was shocked to see him at a church meeting. She was torn inside but knew that she had to forgive this man, despite his evil past. It was an extreme example of offering grace to another person. Corrie realized that by forgiving the guard, she was doing as much for her own self as she was him. When we hold grudges or intern our anger even on small matters, we are tearing ourselves up inside. By offering someone grace and moving on with our life, we relieve ourselves of tremendous stress and pressure. We are doing as much good for ourselves as we are for our neighbor.

Another significant way we can be a good neighbor is "Paying it Forward". This concept has bounced around through history, possibly starting with Ralph Waldo Emerson. As a graduate of The Ohio State University (should the THE be in all caps), I learned this lesson from Woody Hayes. He was the legendary football coach of the Buckeyes from 1951-1978. He was the head coach that my father's generation looked to as an example of toughness. His football philosophy was "three yards and a cloud of dust". Meaning, you run the ball hard at your opponent and try to beat them down physically. (I delivered mail to his widow's house several times after college.) He was one of the first college coaches to actively recruit African American players and hire them to coach alongside him. Rex Kern (one of his famous quarterbacks) would tell stories of Coach Hayes standing with the students during campus protests in the 1970s.

During my first freshman year at Ohio State, at the 1986 commencement, he gave a speech. Part of it involved "Paying it Forward". "I would like to start out with something that I use in almost every speech, and that is the idea of paying forward. Paying forward- that is the thing that you folks with your great education from here can do for the rest of your lives... Take that attitude towards life, because so seldom can we pay back those whom you owe- your parents and other people will be gone. Emerson had something to say about that. He said, 'you can pay back seldom, but you can always pay forward'."

There was also a movie made about it in 2000 called "Pay it Forward". The film showed the concept sweeping the globe and changing the world. It could change our world, but it needs to start with individuals willing to make small changes.

So, how can we pay it forward? Loving your neighbor is a great start. We could help those in need everywhere we go. Donate to worthy charities. When my father was young, a local charity called Charity Newsies would give him clothes to wear to school. I can't pay them back for what they did for him, but I will surely be handing them money every year to help the next generation. We can support people emotionally as well as financially. We can pray for others and let them know that we really care about their wellbeing. We can sit down with them and listen instead of judging them from afar.

Throughout history, most of our conflicts arise because we simply don't love our neighbors. Wars begin because we want someone else's land, resources or simple hatred. There has probably been no greater evil in history than slavery. Image taking someone from their home, shipping them thousands of miles away, and enslaving them to do your work. We can't pay someone back for this injustice, so we need to pay forward. We can make it our goal every day to try harder to love our neighbor. We can offer them grace and pay it forward for further generations.

CHAPTER 12

YOU ARE AWESOME

"Love you neighbor as yourself", will it work if we don't love ourselves? Oftentimes, the world, social media, our friends and family can make it tough to love ourselves. We may feel like everyone is judging us as failures. "You are not as smart as your sister", "You're not as athletic as your brother", "Why can't you be like the others?". It can all be so overwhelming. Maybe you aren't perfect. Newsflash, no one else is perfect either. We all have our flaws. So, we will all have to attack life with what we have been provided.

The first thing that you really need to grab onto is this: You are Awesome! God created you to be exactly who you are. He spoke the rest of creation into being, but he made humans with his own hands. So basically, what I am saying is, God still thinks that we are worth his time and energy. He will stop and listen to your prayers, your problems, and your concerns. If it is important to you, it is important to him. Think about that, you are so special that the creator of the universe listens to what you have to say.

"But I've done so many things wrong." We all have screwed up and do you know what's most important: You're Forgiven. Just ask God and it's forgiven. He wipes it off our slate and doesn't look back. Remember how we are expected to "keep no record of wrongs". God is willing to delete your sin history. We need to be able to do the same thing for ourselves and others. Do you remember the scene from the movie "The Lion King"? The scene where Rafiki slaps Simba with his stick. He tells Simba that it doesn't matter anymore because it's in his past. Simba says that it still hurts and Rafiki reminds him that the past can hurt but he must move on.

You were put on the earth for a purpose. We are all part of the body of Christ and have a roll to play. We just need to figure out what our part is. Maybe it's to be a great parent or aunt or uncle. Maybe you'll cure cancer, become a great plumber, or figure out how to make television commercials quieter. It might take a lifetime to find you niche, so we might have to be patient with ourselves. We all have an important part to play in life's drama. We are all essential.

You can inspire so many others by living your life to its fullest. It's true that we have all squandered precious time, but we can start anew today. The past is behind us, so let's leave it there. Give someone else a high-five today and inspire them to be their best self. You can even give yourself a high-five and remind yourself how awesome you truly are. We tend to be our worst critics. I'm reminding us all to "give ourselves a break". Stand up to the doubts in your own mind and the ones you face daily from others. You can be there for yourself and your doubters. Availability may be the greatest ability ever created. Be available for others and try to inspire them to make each day better than the one before. Years of coaching has shown me how often the players look across the field for their parents and friends. Be there for them and everyone who needs your support. Maybe that is why you were created, to be an encourager. The world needs a lot more of them. Your neighbor needs your love as much as you need it. Believe in yourself. You are awesome, forgiven, important, and inspiring. You are worthy of being loved and giving love to your neighbors.

CHAPTER 13

CHANGE THE WORLD

Thousands of years of history have taught us a lot. The problem is, it has also taught politicians and political action committees as well. They have learned how to divide us. They like to put us into separate groups and pit us against each other. And you know what, they have gotten their way too many times. Dividing us helps mobilize their electorate and gets millions donated to their causes. If they can make us think that our rights or opinions are being trampled on, then we send them money. The results are devastating: More division and less loving our neighbor.

We need to stop listening to them and look around. We all live on the same small planet. We are all a lot more alike than we want to admit. God created every one of us for a purpose and I'm sure it was not to hate others. I remember hearing the phrase, "God doesn't make junk". It's true. You know what, he loves us. Maybe that needs to be stressed more. HE LOVES US!!! I could not write this essay without including this verse. Jeremiah 29:11 "For I know the plans I have for you, declares the Lord, plans to prosper you and not to harm you, plans to give you hope and a future." God has good things planned for us, but sometimes we need to get out of the way.

We tend to stress our differences instead of our similarities. We need to stop allowing ourselves to be divided by politicians or social media as they prey on our differences. Remember what Benjamin Franklin said, "We must, indeed, all hang together or most assuredly we shall all hang separately." The best way to prevent this from happening is to work together, we can change things through our own actions. One person can make a difference, and it can be you. We need to try and be optimistic about everything. We can look for the good in others and praise it. We can help change other's lives for the better and it will change us as well. I've heard it said, "You can't change them." If one negative player can bring down a team, then one positive person can lift them up.

As a mail carrier, carrying mail in the Midwest during winter can be tough. As March approaches, I find myself looking for the little yellow flowers in the grass along my route. (I'm talking about the McKenzie's' yard on Kioka Avenue, if you live on my route) Those little insignificant yellow flowers springing from the ground inspire me. They remind me that spring is coming. We can all be these little yellow flowers in someone else's life. We can inspire them or show them that someone cares about their life and successes. I will admit that when someone on my route opens the door and asks me to sign one of my books; I'm on cloud nine for the rest of the day. We can all do this for someone else if we look for ways to love our neighbor daily.

I used to get irritated with a friend of mine. He would constantly say that he "felt bad" for someone. I would ask him, "what are you going to do about it?" We can't just continually say we "feel bad" and think we have accomplished anything. We need to act. We can do something to help make a positive change. You can support your neighbors through local charities, if you can't support them physically. Groups like the Charity Newsies, foodbanks, and local churches can help you "pay it forward". You can also help your neighbors thousands of miles away through charities like the Salvation Army, World Vision, and many others. They can serve as your surrogate and offer care for the neighbors you can't see from your front door.

There are probably plenty of churches in your area that would love to put you to work caring for those in need. I know, "I can't go to church until I get my life right." God said I forgive you, so let's move on. Romans 5:8 says, "While we were still sinners,

Christ died for us." He has already performed the sacrifice for us. I promise you that there are a great deal of churches waiting for you to take a seat to praise and serve God with them.

We have made great progress as citizens of earth. We don't close schools down to separate races anymore. We don't accept the enslavement of others. We have come very far but have a long way to go. We must unify as one people and learn to: "Love the Lord your God with all your heart and with all your soul and with all your mind and with all your strength." And then, "Love your neighbor as yourself." If we just take that simple task to heart, we can change the world for the better a little more each day. We can make tomorrow a better day together. We need to follow the great examples from history like Mother Theresa, Dr. Martin Luther King Jr., Reverend Billy Graham, and many others. We can make a difference if the lives of our neighbors. Love God and love our neighbors. When we start to approach life this way, we can change history.

ABOUT THE AUTHOR

James D Bethel

James is a part time author and a full time Christian husband and father. He has been carrying mail for 30 years for the U.S. Postal Service. As his mind wanders on his route, he creates stories in his mind. He occasionally writes them down. This time he has tried his hand at a non-fiction essay.

BOOKS BY THIS AUTHOR

A Race For The Crown

Fiction novel. Join a government employee, a Catholic priest, and their family and friends as they race through time and history to track down Jesus's Crown of Thorns before the Russian mafia, ISIS, or the President of the United States can plunder it for their own gain.

Find Your Way Home

Fiction novel. A small town trailkeeper is recruited by the CIA to undertake a simple mission overseas. Once in Iran, the operation goes sideways. He has to find enough faith and courage to walk his way through hostile territory and find his way back home.

Made in the USA
Middletown, DE
29 October 2022

13759325R00033